Enjoy Your Build Process!

An Insider's Guide

To Confident Custom Home Building with Tips, Strategies, and Checklists

Joseph K. Keresztury

Our Complimentary Custom Home Building Checklist available at: CustomHome411.com

Contents

Introduction…
thinking of building?

Hello there, I hope you're sitting comfortably, possibly with a strong cup of coffee by your side, or perhaps a glass of your preferred vintage, because we're about to embark on quite an adventure! You're about to dive into the enthralling world of custom home building, and by the end of this literary journey, I hope you'll not only feel more confident about it, but also be somewhat entertained. Because let's face it, the journey of building a home is much like a classic sit-com. You've got the twists, the turns, and, of course, the bloopers. But much like the best TV shows, in the end, it's the journey and the end result that make it all worthwhile!

I hear you asking, "Wait a minute, did you just compare building my dream home to a sitcom?" Why, yes. Yes, I did. There will be moments of intense planning that rival the strategy meetings of the "Friends" gang at Central Perk. Your discussions with designers and builders may sometimes feel as mind-boggling as a conversation in the "Big Bang Theory." And, yes, there will likely be instances that seem to come straight from the slapstick of "Home Improvement."

But don't worry! That's where this book comes in.

Disclaimer (What This Book Is Not)

Now, before we strap on our metaphorical hard hats and delve into the labyrinth of home building, let's be clear about what this book is, and, equally important, what it isn't.

Firstly, and with all due respect to your ambitions, this book is not going to turn you into a seasoned site supervisor or construction manager mogul overnight. The nitty-gritty of running a building business or construction site, such as scheduling, material sourcing, wrangling sub-contractors, budgeting, funding, quality control, code compliance, and project management, are topics beyond the scope of this tome. To unravel those would need the literary equivalent of the Great Wall of China, and years to digest. So, if you're acting as an owner-builder, we might not delve into the minutiae of your role, but fear not, we do offer full consulting services if needed.

What this book aims to be is your trusty umbrella in the wild weather of the custom home building process. I'm here to provide an overview based on real-world experience, to help you navigate the inevitable rainstorms and maybe even dance in the rain a bit. We'll guide you around the common potholes and show you the scenic routes, with a handy checklist, key factors, steps, and proven methods to ensure that your custom home is as unique and rewarding as your favorite TV show's season finale.

Primarily, this book is a simple, direct, and effective resource that focuses on the things you probably care most about. After all, we understand that your interests are more likely to center around the magnificent view from your kitchen or the convenience of an outlet by your nightstand, rather than the specifications of a nail or the exact schedule of a stone mason.

Enjoy Your Build Process!

The goal? To help you enjoy your build process as much as you will enjoy your custom home. So, grab another cup of coffee or refill that wine glass. Let's get to work on building not just your dream home, but also some great memories in the process.

Section 1

13 Tips to Dodge Costly Surprises and Tear-Your-Hair-Out Moments

Brace yourself, my friend, because we're about to embark on a thrilling ride, a rollercoaster of a journey called home building. Yes, you heard it right. Thrilling, exciting, adventurous, and believe it or not, a heck of a lot of fun!

Picture this: You, standing proudly at the doorstep of your beautiful, newly-built custom home. Every brick, every beam, every window - they all tell a story. A story of persistence, hard work, a couple of face-palms, hearty laughs, maybe a tear or two, and ultimately, a whole lot of satisfaction and pride. Quite a vision, right?

But here's the thing. Any epic story worth telling is filled with twists and turns, ups and downs. The same goes for your custom home building adventure.

However, equipped with the right set of tools (or in our case, tips), you can navigate this journey much more confidently and efficiently.

So, welcome to Chapter 1 - a baker's dozen of our very best advice, tips, and tricks to help you avoid those pesky pitfalls and unanticipated headaches. A comprehensive guide that will arm you with insights and strategies to make your home building journey more rewarding and even, dare we say it, enjoyable! So, grab your hard hat (metaphorically, of course) and let's get started!

#1 - Adapting your Dream Castle to the Real World

You've got your eye on this plot, right? And your blueprint practically sings "Home Sweet Home." But, my friend, the actual site could be singing a different tune. Picture this: your favorite cup of coffee in your hands, early morning, and you're walking the lot with your builder. You're analyzing the sun's path, double-checking with the HOA's list of do's and don'ts, discussing water drainage, eyeing those picturesque views, considering utilities, and even getting a feel for where the driveway might sit. Just like making sure your socks match before leaving the house, you're aligning your plans to your lot.

#2 - Laying the Foundation without Breaking the Bank

Here's the thing about construction costs: just like a sneaky calorie-packed dessert, some items hit your budget harder than you think. Utilities, foundations, and framing, my friend, are the cheesecakes of homebuilding costs. A support post on your patio or between windows, for instance, could save you the cost of expensive beams. If you're installing a septic system or a water well, they need to find room in your budget. It's all about using those cost-effective measures to prevent your finances from getting, let's say, "waistline problems."

#3 - Buddy Up with Your Builder

Think about the closest people in your life. Good communication is the secret, right? Well, guess what, it's no different when you're building your dream home. Working with a builder who's more buddy than builder can make the difference between a sitcom and a horror show. Open communication doesn't mean you're glued to your phone 24/7. Set up some structure. We use a build software with client app called BuilderTrend, which provides a platform for regular updates during the build process. It's like the weekly news, but only about your home and, thankfully, with fewer commercials.

#4 - Expect the Unexpected

Hate to break it to you, but building a home is not like ordering a pizza. There will be times when things go awry - bad weather, a sick contractor, a broken compressor - and your house won't be ready in 30 minutes or less. You can't be a perfectionist in this process unless you fancy joining the Hair Loss Club. Remember, quality over speed, just like cooking your grandma's secret spaghetti sauce.

#5 - Time Isn't Always on Your Side

Wouldn't it be great if we could set an exact date for our house to be ready, like booking a vacation?

Reality check: anyone who tells you this is probably selling you a fairy tale. Let's work with a "time frame" instead, something like "early summer" or "before the holidays." Once the cabinets are in place, we can start marking dates on the calendar. Oh, and don't forget to account for pre-construction items too.

#6 - Make it Visual.

Remember the childlike joy of drawing your dream house? Well, adulthood doesn't mean we stop doing that. Use vision boards, technology, samples - anything that helps you see your plans before they're carved in stone. And don't forget to step on your plot with the blueprint in hand. Walk, measure, feel the space. It's like a dress rehearsal for your home.

#7 - Keep an 'Idea' Binder

Here's something fun: Start an 'idea' binder. Include everyone in the family, even the family dog if he's got an opinion. It can be a mood board of your dream house. It's fun, it's useful, and most importantly, it keeps everyone on the same page - literally!

#8 - Prioritize Your Budget

Budgeting for a home is like packing for a trip. You've got items you can't do without (passport, tickets) and those you can buy or replace (toothpaste, clothes). Your budget should prioritize things you can't change easily after construction. Those chic garage doors can wait; ensuring the fireplace is perfect can't.

Pro Tip: **Future proof for potential longer-term items.**

#9 - Say Cheese before Closing Up the Walls

Think of this as the behind-the-scenes footage of your house. Just as a director takes B-roll shots, take a video before the drywall is up. You'll have an 'x-ray' vision of your house, making future changes much easier.

#10 - A Closet Isn't Just a Closet

In the midst of all the excitement, don't forget about closets and storage space. It's like leaving the house and realizing you forgot your wallet. So, make sure you're planning for enough storage spaces.

#11 - It's Not All About Bricks and Mortar

You know what they say, "All work and no play...". Well, in this case, "all construction and no furnishings...". You're going to have additional costs, like moving expenses, furniture, and even landscaping. So, make sure you budget for these too.

#12 - Get an Extra Pair of Eyes

A good builder will welcome a third-party inspection. It's like having a proofreader for your thesis. They're a fresh pair of eyes that can pick up on things we might miss. It's not about doubting your builder; it's about ensuring everything's within compliance.

#13 - Stay Local

When it comes to builders and their trades, think local. They're more accountable, familiar with the area, and easier to call upon if things go south. It's like having your favorite restaurant just around the corner - comforting and convenient.

Pro Tip!

Get a detailed spec sheet before construction starts. It's your roadmap to understanding where your money is going and what to do if things change. A good builder will also offer suggestions upfront to help cut down your budget, just like a good friend helping you choose the right outfit for a date.

And there you have it! My 13 pearls of wisdom, with a bonus thrown in. Follow these, and you'll be on your way to an exciting, rewarding, and surprisingly entertaining home building journey. Buckle up, and let's get started!

Section 1.2

Mastering the Expectations Triangle

Welcome to the Bermuda Triangle of Expectations

Ever heard of the Bermuda Triangle? It's that mysterious region where ships and aircraft are said to have disappeared under peculiar circumstances. Well, we're about to embark on a journey through an equally enigmatic territory, but instead of ships and planes, we're dealing with Budget, Functionality, and Personalization. It's the Bermuda Triangle of custom home building, where without careful navigation, dreams may disappear!

Budget

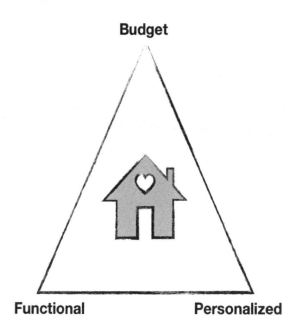

Functional   **Personalized**

#1: The Dollars and Cents of Home Building: Budget

Let's imagine your budget is an all-you-can-eat buffet. Now, we all know how these buffets work, right? Your eyes are always bigger than your stomach. The endless choices are tempting, but here's the hard truth: you can't pile everything on your plate without feeling a little sick later. Similarly, a limited budget doesn't allow for gold-plated faucets in every bathroom or marble countertops in the laundry room. The key is to make informed choices based on your budget buffet and remember, indigestion in the form of budget blowouts is not fun!

#2: The Backbone of Your Dream Home: Functionality

Think of functionality as the skeleton of your home. It's what holds everything together and gives your house its basic shape. It doesn't matter how luxurious your curtains are if you have no windows to hang them on, right? Functionality is about the essentials, the structural must-haves. It's like showing up at a potluck with chips and dip but forgetting the chips. You need both for the whole thing to make sense!

#3: Making Your House Your Home: Personalization

Personalization is the spice of your home – it's what makes it uniquely yours. It's the cherry on top, the salsa dance in a world of waltz, the color to your black and white movie. But remember, just like too much chili can make your favorite taco inedible, too much personalization without consideration of the budget and functionality can lead to a beautiful but impractical house. Or worse, an over-personalized home that's hard to sell later.

Navigating Through the Triangle: The Balancing Act

It's important to give equal attention to each corner of this triangle. Neglecting one for the others is like trying to sit on a two-legged stool - you're bound to fall flat on your face! For instance, if you spend all your budget on personalized luxuries, you might find yourself with a gold-plated bathtub in a house without a roof. Or, if you focus too much on functionality, you might end up with a house that looks and feels like a sterile hospital room.

The Time-Budget Connection: Quick Jet or Slow Train?

Now, let's throw time into the mix. You see, the time frame for your home build is indirectly proportional to your budget. Imagine you need to travel from Dallas to Miami. Sure, you could get there in a couple of hours in a private jet, but that would cost you an arm and a leg. On the other hand, you could take a 13-day train ride at a fraction of the cost, but do you really have that much time (and patience)?

Finding the sweet spot in home building is similar. It's like choosing a straight flight with no layovers – it's not as quick as a private jet, not as slow as a train, but it gets you there in reasonable time, comfort, and cost. The same applies to your home build - you need to balance your budget, time frame, and external factors.

Aiming for the Sky, Landing Among the Stars

Remember, we're building a custom home, not chasing unicorns. The goal here is not perfection - after all, whose definition of 'perfect' are we using? Instead, focus on maintaining standards within realistic expectations. Identify what's most important to you and make sure they are respected in all three components of the triangle.

Enjoy Your Build Process!

Navigating the Expectations Triangle isn't easy, but with a little patience and a lot of careful planning, you can sail through this journey smoothly. Remember, like any good journey, it's all about balance. So, put on your captain's hat, grab your navigation chart, and let's set sail towards your dream home!

Section 2

Before the First Nail: Navigating Pre-Construction

Welcome to the Maze of Pre-Construction

Imagine you're about to run a marathon, but instead of warming up, you decide to wing it and jump straight to the starting line. How far do you think you'll get before you're huffing and puffing, regretting not lacing your shoes properly or missing that last sip of water? Building a home is a marathon, not a sprint, and what happens before the construction can be the critical difference between a successful project and a house of horrors.

Unlocking the Gate: Lot / Land Development

First things first: you've got your land. Your piece of paradise. But right now, it's just a patch of wilderness. It needs to be cleared and prepped. This stage is like getting a haircut before a big event. You've got to trim the excess to present the best possible version. Clearing a lot may seem straightforward, but remember to consider the removal of debris and brush – you can't just stuff it in a closet and pretend it doesn't exist!

The Veins of Your Home: Utilities Assessment

Next up is utilities. These are the veins and arteries of your home, providing essential services like water and electricity. Think of this as setting up the kitchen for a big dinner. You wouldn't start cooking without knowing if you have a functioning stove or enough pots and pans, right? Assessing utilities, from whether they are available to how they'll enter your home, is essential. Remember, utilities are pretty much the driving force to your home - they need a point of entry and a path of least resistance.

The Jigsaw Puzzle: Site Placement

Now, let's talk about your house's position on your land. This is like playing a giant jigsaw puzzle with your home as the central piece. You need to consider the lay of the land, the best views, and any easements or setbacks. Getting this right can mean the difference between waking up to a glorious sunrise over the lake or to a view of your neighbor's unattractive backyard gnome collection.

The Game Plan: Budget

Let's move on to your budget. Knowing your numbers is crucial. It's like planning a grocery list before shopping: you don't want to wander aimlessly down the aisles, throwing random items into your cart. You need to reverse engineer your plans, design, and specifications to match your budget. This helps avoid disappointment while ensuring your "must-haves" are met. A balanced budget is like a balanced diet, you get to enjoy the good stuff without overindulging and suffering the consequences later.

Blueprint of Dreams: Floor Plan and Design

Now, it's time to translate your dreams into a blueprint, the script for your home's story. This process is like creating a playlist for a party - you want the right mix of songs to set the mood and keep your guests entertained. Remember, it's crucial to involve your builder early in this process. It's like having a DJ who knows how to read the room - they can guide you, minimize miscommunications, and help you stay in tune with your budget and requirements.

The Shopping List: Specification Sheet

The specification sheet is your home's shopping list. It's the difference between baking a delicious cake and a forgettable one. It breaks down the materials and methods, outlining what's included (and what's not!). It's also vital for your suppliers, trades, and field crews – they'll base their scope of work on this. The specification sheet is like the recipe for your home. And we all know what happens when we skip parts of the recipe!

Funding: Financing

Next up, financing. It's always wise to get pre-approved upfront so you can plan better. Just like you wouldn't leave home without checking your wallet, you need to have a clear understanding of your financial commitments to avoid any unpleasant surprises later.

The Red Tape: Permits / HOA Approvals

The next step is permits and HOA approvals. This is like the security checkpoint at the airport - without the right documents, you're not going anywhere. It might be a bit of a hassle, but it's better than being grounded!

The Backbone: Engineering

Engineering is your home's backbone, providing structural integrity and stability. This is particularly crucial for the foundation. You wouldn't build a sandcastle close to the shoreline, would you? The same principle applies here. Your home needs a strong foundation to stand firm and last long.

The Timeline: Construction Phase Schedule

Having a construction phase schedule is like having a detailed itinerary for a road trip. It outlines milestones and provides a general timeframe so you can plan accordingly. It's not just about knowing when you'll reach your destination, but also when to make essential stops along the way.

The Fine Details: Selections

Making selections is like choosing the color of your car or the toppings on your pizza. These choices lend uniqueness to your custom home. Remember, early decisions prevent unnecessary delays - no one wants their pizza delivered cold!

The Blueprint for Success: Build Package

Finally, you'll likely need a complete "build package" for your lender. It's like the directions for assembling that complicated piece of IKEA furniture. With clear instructions, you'll avoid confusion and unnecessary delays. This package will also paint the picture for a completed homes that the bank appraisal will base his appraisal on.

Breathe in, breathe out. I know it's a lot to take in, but remember, your builder is your ally through this maze. With a good sense of humor and a pocketful of patience, you're well on your way to transforming your dream into a reality.

Section 2.2

The ABC's: Deciphering the Price Tag of Your Dream Home

Tackling the Elephant in the Room: The Price

One of the first, and undoubtedly most crucial questions you'll ask is, "How much will it cost to build my custom home?" It's like asking how long is a piece of string. With so many variables, it's a challenge to give a one-size-fits-all answer. But fear not, dear reader, we are going to unravel this knotty question together.

The Custom Build Puzzle: Variables and Cost

Picture a custom home like a gourmet meal. Your price will depend on the ingredients you choose. Do you want a simple, comforting spaghetti Bolognese, or are you after a Michelin-star-worthy Bouillabaisse? Adjustments like tweaking the house's position on your lot or pruning unnecessary construction items can transform your gourmet dreams into a deliciously affordable reality.

The Per Square Foot Mirage: Why it's Not Always Reliable

Many folks think a custom home's cost can be calculated using a simple 'price per square foot' formula. Unfortunately, it's not that simple. Let's think about this in terms of pies. Two pies might have the same diameter, but one could be an apple pie and the other a meat pie. They have the same size, but different ingredients, preparation, and, consequently, different prices. The same is true for houses. Two houses might have the same square footage, but differ significantly in features like roofing, cabinetry, or the number of windows.

Getting a Ballpark Figure: Trust Your Local Builder

Like a good coach, an experienced local builder can give you an idea of the ballpark in which you're playing. They can help you reverse engineer your plans to make your budget work for you. Always remember, not all builders (and spec sheets) are created equal. It's like going on a date - you want someone who values you, respects your needs, and makes you feel special.

The ABCs of Pricing: Simple but Significant

Let's explore this further with the ABCs of home pricing.

A. The Gourmet Home: Imagine a house that has it all - top-of-the-line finishes, state-of-the-art technology, and unique, industry-leading materials. It's like dining at a five-star restaurant, where the dishes are exquisitely crafted, using the best ingredients, cooked to perfection.

B. The High-Value Home: Picture a robust, efficient home that meets your expectations and doesn't compromise on quality. It might not have gold-plated faucets, but it checks off most of your boxes and finds happy compromises on some. Think of it as dining at your favorite local restaurant that delivers great food consistently, offers good value, and keeps you coming back for more.

C. The Functional Home: Visualize a functional home that meets code requirements and passes inspections. It allows for some personal selections and could be termed a "semi-custom" home. It's like a home-cooked meal that may not have fancy ingredients but still satisfies your hunger and tastes good.

D. The Red Flag Home: If a builder offers you a home that seems too good to be true, it probably is! You might be lured by the low prices, but the quality of construction could leave you with a sinking home and a sinking heart. It's like ordering from a questionable fast-food joint - you might end up with a case of bad indigestion!

Options A, B, and C can all result in fantastic homes that you'll cherish for a lifetime. However, they can have the same square footage but wildly different prices. Understanding these differences can help you make an informed decision, align your expectations, and ensure you get the most bang for your buck.

- **Remember,** building a custom home is an investment. It's your hard-earned money. So, do your homework, ask the right questions, and ensure that you're getting the best value for your money. The journey might seem overwhelming, but with the right knowledge, guidance, and a touch of humor, you'll be unlocking the front door of your dream home before you know it!

Section 3

The Roadmap to Your Dream Home: Site-walks - Milestone Checklist

Welcome, to section 3 - our "Sherpa" once construction has commenced on this home building expedition, the guide to milestone walks that make up your journey. Remember when you were a kid, and road trips felt like forever, but those "Are we there yet?" queries were often quelled by interesting pit stops? Think of this chapter as your 'scenic spots' guide. It's time to dive into the exciting adventure of home building, keeping our eyes peeled for these crucial milestones.

Site walk #1 - Site Placement: Picking the Perfect Spot for Your Dream Home

Site placement is like planning a picnic - you scout the park, find the perfect spot under a tree with a great view, away from the anthill, and close to the restrooms. It's all about the details and understanding how they will impact your overall experience.

Setting the Stage: House Placement

Firstly, let's talk about house placement. Imagine your lot is a stage, and your house is the star of the show. Your builder is the director, who will guide you on where to position your house to catch the best light, maximize views, and ensure that it doesn't end up with a supporting role!

Clearing the Canvas: Clearing Needed

Next, it's about clearing your canvas, like an artist preparing for their masterpiece. But instead of paint and brushes, we're talking bulldozers and chainsaws. Here's where the pros come in. Your builder will help you determine which trees to keep for privacy, potential views, and to maintain the natural beauty of your lot.

The Invisible Boundaries: Setbacks, Easements, and Envelope

Then come the setbacks and easements - the invisible boundaries of your lot. It's like having an overbearing neighbor who tells you exactly where you can plant your roses. Jokes aside, it's crucial to understand these legal restrictions to avoid future headaches.

The Pathway to Progress: Construction Access Planned Out

Construction access is just as it sounds - how your construction crews will get to and from your building site. This might seem insignificant, but trust me, the last thing you want is a cement truck stuck in your soon-to-be rose garden.

The Lifelines: Utilities Set Up and Planned For

Finally, you need to plan for utilities and have them set up at this point as they will be needed for construction. These are the lifelines of your home, delivering essential services like water, electricity, and internet. It's like planning the plumbing for a giant fish tank - you need to know where the pipes will go, where the filters will be placed, and how it will all come together to create a comfortable environment for your fish (or in this case, your family).

The Unsung Hero: Foundation

With the site placement sorted, the foundation steps into the spotlight. Like a quiet but reliable friend, the foundation supports your home and sets the stage for everything that follows. A well-planned foundation ensures that your house remains sturdy and resilient while functional, providing a safe and secure place for you and your family.

And with that, once foundation poured, you're ready to order the lumber package - the physical embodiment of your dream starting to take shape! Remember, building a home is an exciting journey, and each milestone is a step towards making your dream a reality. So, buckle up and enjoy the ride!

Site walk #2 - The Skeleton of Your Dream: Framing & Pre-Rough-In Walk

Framing is like setting up the skeleton for your dream home. Imagine it as putting together a giant 3D puzzle where each piece plays a crucial role in shaping your home. As exciting as it is to see your house framed up, this stage also signals the start of mechanical rough-ins. Your home will start looking less like a construction site and more like, well, a home!

Windows and Doors: The Eyes and Gateway of Your Home

Just as eyes are the window to your soul, windows are the eyes of your home. They determine the amount of natural light that will illuminate your interiors, the views you'll enjoy, and, to an extent, the energy efficiency of your house. Take time to review all windows and doors. If something doesn't feel right, it's time to consider a change order. Remember, it's easier to change your mind now than to live with regret later.

HVAC Unit Locations: The Breathing Lungs of Your Home

Next up is the HVAC unit - the lungs of your home. Here's where things cool down (or heat up!). Review the locations of your HVAC units inside and out, and ensure they're ideally positioned for function and efficiency.

Flickering Warmth: Fireplace and Mantel / Hearth

For those cozy winter nights, we move to the fireplace and mantel. It's like planning where to set up your campfire for the best warmth and ambiance. Consider the aesthetics, the safety, and the functional aspects when reviewing these features with your builder.

Hidden Passageways: Attic Access Points

Attic access points are your home's hidden passageways. Review these locations for practicality and convenience, because no one wants to play a game of hide and seek when they need to access their attic!

The Oasis: Shower Niches and Valve Locations

Onto the bathroom, where shower niches and valve locations are essential for comfort and functionality. It's like choosing the best spots to place your snacks and drinks when setting up for movie night. You want them accessible, but not in the way!

Water Heartbeat: Water Heater or Softener Locations

Water heaters and softeners are like the heartbeat of your home's water supply. Position them for easy access and maintenance, but out of the way of your day-to-day activities.

Culinary Canvas: Cabinet Layouts

Moving onto the kitchen, cabinet layouts play a crucial role. They're like the stage set-up for your culinary performances. You want them positioned for maximum functionality and aesthetic appeal.

Outdoor Connectivity: Exterior Stub Outs and Hose Bib Locations

Exterior stub outs, access points and hose bib locations are your home's connection to the outdoors. (Future proof where needed) Review these features for gardening convenience, car washing, or summertime water fights!

Supportive Framework: Blocking Locations

Finally, let's talk about blocking locations. These are for supporting fixtures like TVs, curtains, mirrors, and holders. It's like planning where to hang your favorite paintings in an art gallery. You want them in the right spots to optimize viewing and appreciation.

Pro Tip: blocking in the wall will allow you strong anchor points without having to find the stud.

- **Remember** to review any additional features you might want to add. As the saying goes, "Measure twice, cut once." It's far easier to make adjustments at this stage than to realize you've missed something once your home is completed. Your home is a reflection of you, so don't shy away from making it exactly how you want it!

Site walk #3 - Powering Up Your Dream: Electric "Blue Box" Walkthrough

The 'Blue Box' walk might sound like a scene from a sci-fi movie, but it's an essential milestone in your home's construction. This walkthrough happens before electrical rough-ins begin. This phase is like planning a city's layout - deciding where to put the lampposts, the traffic signals, and the power lines. It's incredibly engaging, so get ready to roll up your sleeves!

Switches and Lights: Creating the Ambiance

The first thing to review is the placement of switches and lights. Imagine entering your home at night; where would you want the switches for easy access? Which areas require bright light, and where would you prefer a softer ambiance? Walk around each room and think about how you'll use the space. Remember, what looks good on paper might feel different when you're standing in the room itself.

Outlet Positions: Powering Your Lifestyle

Next, consider the outlet positions. This is like deciding where to put the water coolers in an office -

you want them handy but unobtrusive. Think about your lifestyle - will you be working from home and need multiple outlets for your computer, printer, and coffee maker? Or perhaps you're a foodie who'll use a variety of kitchen appliances? Or maybe you're planning a home theater system that requires specific wiring? Make sure you have an outlet for every possible need, and future-proof your home wherever you can.

Panel Locations: The Heart of Your Home's Electrical System

Panel locations may not be the most exciting part of your home design, but they're like the heart of your home's electrical system. Think of them as the conductor in the orchestra of your electrical system. Their placement should be convenient for maintenance but discreet enough not to be an eyesore.

Navigating Through Structural Adjustments

During your Blue Box walkthrough, keep in mind that you may need to make some adjustments due to the home's structure. Sometimes, a switch might need to be relocated because the studs in the wall don't leave enough space. Like trying to find the perfect spot for your sun lounger on a crowded beach, sometimes adjustments are necessary!

The Comprehensive Pre-Electric / Blue Box Milestone Walk Checklist

We don't have the space here to list everything you need to consider during your Blue Box walkthrough, but don't worry, we've got you covered! Here's a quick taste of what you should look out for:

1. *Double-check that all rooms have enough outlets and switches, taking into account your specific needs for each room.*

2. *Review the positions of ceiling lights, sconces, and other lighting fixtures.*

3. *Verify that all heavy-load appliances have dedicated circuits.*

4. *Confirm that your home's electrical panel is conveniently located.*

5. *Make sure that outdoor outlets, lights, and other electrical features are correctly positioned and weather-proofed.*

6. *Consider tech needs, like charging stations for devices, smart home system integration, and home theater wiring.*

7. *Remember safety features, like GFCI outlets in bathrooms and kitchens, and sufficient smoke detectors.*

Remember, this stage is your chance to ensure your new home will work for you and your lifestyle. It might be a lot to take in, but careful planning now will result in a home that truly feels like it was built just for you!

Site walk #4 –

Adding the Finishing Touches: Trim and Flatwork Walkthrough

Welcome to the 'Trim and Flatwork' stage, the twilight zone of your home building journey. This is when your home starts looking less like a construction site and more like the dream home you've been envisioning. The sweat and dust have started giving way to finer details, and we're about to add some lipstick and rouge to our creation.

The Hidden Storage: All Closets and Shelving

First up, we're going to delve into every nook and cranny. That's right, it's time to review all closets and shelving layouts. Think of your closets like your secret chocolate stash - out of sight but filled with things that bring you joy. Ensure they're configured to accommodate your wardrobe, linens, cleaning supplies, or whatever else you plan to store.

The Glass Gateway: Shower and Mirror Glass

Next, step into the bathroom and focus on the shower and mirror glass. Reflect on your reflection - is it in the right spot? Is the shower glass correctly installed? These features play a significant role in the aesthetics and functionality of your bathroom.

Fine-Tuning: Confirming Fixtures

On to confirming that all fixtures are trimmed out correctly. This is like doing a soundcheck before a concert; you want to make sure everything works as it should. We don't want any electrical guitar solos interrupted because of a faulty amplifier!

Creating Pathways: Review Flatwork Layouts

Moving outside, it's time to review the flatwork layouts, which include your driveway and walkways. Picture these like arteries in the body of your home, guiding your family and guests from the street to your front door or around your property.

Extra Special: Custom Features or Add-Ons

Last but not least, we'll revisit any custom features or add-ons. This might include extra shelving or crown molding. These features are like the cherry on top of your ice cream sundae - the little extras that make your home uniquely yours.

This walkthrough ensures that your home is not just a house but a special haven where you'll create memories, share love, and feel truly at home.

Site walk #5 – Blue Tape Walk

The grand finale!

Get this milestone checklist where you review all items one last time to assure up to expectations, specifications and standards along with the other four milestone checklist in PDF at:

CustomHome411.com

Section 4

Securing Peace of Mind: The Essential Key Phase Inspections

Get ready to dive into the thrilling world of inspections! Welcome to Section 4, where we demystify the process of home inspections and why they're as important as a seat belt on a roller coaster ride. No one wants to lose sleep wondering if they made the right choices during their home build. And let's be real, you deserve sweet dreams in your new dream home, not nightmares about whether you've crossed all your Ts and dotted your Is!

Laying a Strong Foundation: Pre-Pour Inspection

Let's start from the ground up with the first inspection: the foundation or pre-pour. Imagine laying the foundation is like making the crust for a cheesecake. It needs to be solid, stable, and prepared correctly, or the whole dessert could crumble. Your home is no different! A solid foundation sets the stage for everything else, and a pre-pour inspection ensures it's prepared correctly.

Creating the Structure: Framing Inspection

Once your home's foundation is solid, it's time to frame up. Think of this like assembling a large LEGO set. The framing outlines the shape of your home and creates its basic structure. Just like you wouldn't want to find out you're missing a LEGO piece only after you've nearly completed the set, you wouldn't want to discover a problem with your home's frame when you're ready to move in. This inspection checks that all the "building blocks" of your home are in place and correctly assembled, including rough-ins.

The Finish Line: Final Inspection

The final inspection is like the dress rehearsal before a play. This inspection makes sure that all systems are a go, and everything is ready for the big day when you get your keys. Just as you wouldn't want any flubbed lines or missing props on opening night, you don't want any surprises when you move into your new home.

Going the Extra Mile: Pre-Drywall Review

Tip, there should be a general pre-drywall review. This review is a final 'sneak peek' at your home before all the interior walls are sealed up. It's the last opportunity to make any change orders to electrical outlets, plumbing

lines, or other features that will be hidden behind the drywall without it being a major project. Yes, it's the chance to ensure there's an outlet right beside your bed for that charging phone or reading lamp!

- **Remember,** these inspections are your safeguard, your assurance that your dream home is not only beautiful but also well-built and safe. So go ahead, breathe that sigh of relief and look forward to peaceful nights in your new home, knowing that every detail has been meticulously inspected and approved.

Section 4.1

From Ground to Gorgeous: The Actual Journey of Your Home Build (Actual Construction)

Getting ready to break ground is like standing at the starting line of an exciting marathon – adrenaline is high, and the anticipation is palpable. But what exactly lies ahead? Here's a snapshot review of your upcoming journey, from the first shovel of dirt to the gleaming, polished finishes.

1. Crafting the Plan

Like a treasure map guiding you to the hidden bounty, the planning stage is where we chart the course for the journey ahead. This phase is all about strategizing, ensuring we have the right materials, and confirming that all elements of the design are ready to go.

2. Site Preparation and Foundation Laying

This stage is the 'first dig', where your plot of land starts transforming into the site of your future home.

It involves clearing the land, setting out the footprint of the house, and laying the foundation - the bedrock upon which your home will rest.

3. Framing the Dream

Now, we start giving shape to your home by building the frame - its skeleton, if you will. This phase is like a 3D jigsaw puzzle, with beams and posts interlocking to outline the rooms and spaces of your home. You'll start to see the real size and scale of your dream dwelling.

4. Rough-Ins & Roof

Next up, we install the rough-ins - the behind-the-scenes heroes of your home. These include electrical wiring, plumbing lines, and HVAC ductwork. Around the same time, the roof goes up, shielding the inner workings from the elements.

5. Putting Up the Walls

Once the rough-ins are in place, we insulate and drywall the interior and give it the first coat of paint.

This stage is like watching an artist fill in an outline on a canvas - you start to get a real sense of the final picture.

6. Filling in the Details

Now, we turn our attention to the details that make a house a home. We install cabinets and countertops, lay tile and flooring, and transform rooms from construction zones into livable spaces.

7. Trimming and Fine-tuning

This stage, known as the 'trim-out', is where the fixtures, trim, and interior doors go in. It's like accessorizing an outfit - adding earrings here, a belt there - to complete the look.

8. Powering Up and Paving

We're almost there! Now we connect utilities, install appliances, and pour flatwork such as driveways or walkways. It's like putting batteries in a new toy - powering it up and preparing it for action.

9. Finishing Touches

Now we're adding the final touches like hardware, glass, and a second coat of paint. It's like glazing a pottery piece - the last step that brings out the true colors and makes it shine.

10. Perfecting and Polishing

In this final stage, we address any last-minute fixes or 'punch list' items. Then we give everything a thorough cleaning, so your new home is move-in ready. It's like giving your car a wash and wax before a big road trip — everything is sparkling clean and ready for adventure!

- **Remember,** each home's journey might have some variation, but this snapshot gives you an idea of what to expect. So, buckle up and enjoy the ride as you watch your dream home come to life!

Section 4.2

Your Home Build Questions Answered

Embarking on the journey of building your own home is thrilling but it's only natural that you'll have a flurry of questions buzzing in your mind. Don't worry, you're not alone in this. I've curated some of the most frequently asked questions and answered them as if we were sharing a coffee, discussing your upcoming home build project.

Why do I need to make selections so early?

Think of your custom home as a one-of-a-kind concert. Each phase is a band member, and your selections are the sheet music. We need everyone playing the right notes at the right time. Just like a guitar player can't play without strings, a tiler can't start work without the chosen tiles.

Selections vs Allowance Items - What's the difference?

Imagine you're choosing an ice-cream flavor. Selections are like the classic flavors - vanilla, chocolate, and strawberry. They are tried and tested, always available options that you choose from. Allowance items, on the other hand, are like the special flavors, a limited budget is set, and you have the freedom to choose any flavor you desire within that budget.

What about plan adjustments in the field?

A custom home is a symphony of many parts and sometimes, some notes need to be adjusted. It's like composing music – the notes look perfect on paper, but once the orchestra starts to play, you might need to adjust a note here and there for harmony. This doesn't affect the melody; it enhances it.

Pro Tip: drawings or "concepts" on paper do not always correlate to real world construction and feasibility.

How long will it take?

Ah, the million-dollar question! If home-building were a journey, this is asking, "Are we there yet?" The truth is, until we reach the stage where the walls are complete, it's hard to give a precise estimate. It's like baking - you can't know exactly when the bread will rise, but once it's in the oven, you have a better idea.

Why is no one working on-site?

This question is akin to wondering why the magician isn't on stage yet when the show has just begun. A lot of the magic happens behind the scenes, with planning, coordination, and logistics. Also, you wouldn't want a half-baked cake out of the oven, right? So, let's let our trades and vendors do their job fully before moving to the next step.

When will the house be locked up?

Think of the garage doors as the last layer of icing on the cake. It usually happens after the walls are up, textured, painted, and the countertops are in and trim out has started. It's like wrapping a gift before the celebration - you wouldn't want to do it too early or too late!

Can I visit the build site?

Visiting the build site is like walking into a lion's den - it can be thrilling but also dangerous. It's advisable to visit during scheduled site walks or give advance notice.

Pro Tip: be careful not to step / drive on any nails or touch anything - consider it a 'look but don't touch' museum.

Why is the build site 'dirty'?

Remember how your kitchen looks when you're halfway through baking cookies? That's what a build site looks like in between cleanings. Just as you wouldn't worry about flour on the counter while you're still adding ingredients, don't worry about construction debris mid-build. There will or should be planned cleans inside and out in sequence according to phases.

Why do I need to pay for change orders?

Consider a change order as ordering a latte when you've already paid for a black coffee. The change might seem minor, but it affects several other components and hence, costs more. All change orders have a *chain or domino* effect.

Will my house be inspected?

Absolutely! Just as a teacher reviews a final paper, we have in-house and third-party inspections at multiple stages to ensure that every detail is just right.

What is the 'Blue tape' process?

Imagine you're proofreading a final document for typos. The blue tape process is similar - it's your chance to mark anything that needs attention before the final handoff.

When can I move in?

Moving in is like enjoying a perfectly baked pie - you don't want to rush it. It's wise to wait for final inspections, blue tape walks, and a thorough clean to ensure your new home is move-in ready. Because let's face it, a well-baked pie is always worth the wait.

Enjoy Your Build Process!

This sums up some of the most common questions I've come across. Building your home is a remarkable journey so take a deep breath, sit back, and enjoy the process of seeing your dream home come to life.

Conclusion

Your Custom Home Journey: An Unforgettable Symphony

You've made it to the final page, and just as when you close the door to your newly built custom home for the first time, I hope you're filled with a sense of achievement. Building a custom home is a journey, a voyage filled with the ebb and flow of decision-making, teamwork, patience, and triumph. It's like composing a symphony, a complex yet harmonious blend of multiple instruments that culminates in a melody that resonates with your soul.

Building a custom home is not a solo expedition. It's like creating a blockbuster movie – you are the director, but you need a solid crew behind the scenes to make your vision a reality. From a trusted builder to architects and designers' sub-contractors, professional trades, suppliers and site laborers, every team member's role is vital. It's not just a project, but a passionate effort, blending various skills, knowledge, and expertise to create a home that's uniquely yours.

Expectations and communication are the golden threads weaving through the fabric of this process. They're like the lighthouse guiding the ship – helping navigate through uncertainties and challenges, keeping the journey on track. When managed effectively, these two elements can turn a potentially stressful endeavor into a rewarding and enjoyable experience.

Remember, no two custom home journeys are the same, just as no two melodies can be identical. Yours will be unique, echoing your dreams, preferences, and personal touch. This book aims to be your compass, guiding you through the thrilling voyage of building your custom home.

The key to avoiding stress and feeling overwhelmed? -Break it down. Picture the journey like a multi-course meal. You wouldn't devour all the courses at once, would you? Each course is savored one at a time, and so should each phase of your build. Embrace the process, relish in the progress, and let the anticipation of your dream home build with each passing day.

I'm Joseph Keresztury, owner of True Stone Custom Homes, LLC in Texas, a 2nd generation home builder and trusted ally in the wonderful world of custom home building. I've had the pleasure of navigating through numerous custom home journeys in the heart of Texas and offering consulting services across the United States. Our goal is to continue developing the build on your lot experience so you can enjoy the process, we'll handle the rest!

If you'd like our handy Milestone Checklist for your journey, feel free to visit <u>CustomHome411.com</u> to download your complimentary copies in PDF.

To embark on your custom home journey or for consulting services, email me directly at <u>Joseph@TrueStoneHomes.com</u> Our dedicated team is always eager to help you take the first steps towards building your dream home.

Finally, let me leave you with this – building a custom home is like painting on a blank canvas, it's your chance to create a masterpiece. So, dream big, plan well, partner with a good builder and enjoy the process, because the magic lies in the journey as much as the destination. Here's to the beautiful *one-of-a-kind* symphony that will be your custom home!

- **Joseph K.**

Client Driven:

Recommends True Stone Custom Homes

March 31, 2021 · ❧

Joseph has been awesome! He takes the time to listen to the customer wants! I can't wait for my finished custom home!

Fri, Dec 9 at 1:58 PM

...we love our new home and are having kids and grandkids over for our first thanksgiving! You really did a great job in this house. thank you for that.

Thanks so much for meeting ⬛ and me today...everything is coming together nicely! Appreciate your insight and direction in making good decisions! It's gonna look amazing

...r, it will

That's going to look really nice! I appreciate you guys doing that!

Love it

< Back

Mar 17, 2023, 3:20 PM

s (224...

Went by and saw it yesterday. Looks amazing and are so excited. Great progress!

5-star review

Read review

Kassy ⬛

★ ★ ★ ★ ★

TrueStone Custom Home Builders are amazing! The team of Joseph, Kaye, Alex and Nate will take of

Reply to review

Complimentary Checklist: CustomHome411.com

Made in the USA
Las Vegas, NV
18 April 2024

88857073R00039